The
CHRISTMAS CHILD

The
CHRISTMAS CHILD

MAX LUCADO

THOMAS NELSON
Since 1798

NASHVILLE   DALLAS   MEXICO CITY   RIO DE JANEIRO   BEIJING

Published in Nashville, Tennessee, by Thomas Nelson.
Thomas Nelson is a registered trademark of Thomas Nelson, Inc.

Thomas Nelson, Inc., titles may be purchased in bulk for educational, business, fund-raising, or sales promotional use. For information, please e-mail SpecialMarkets@ThomasNelson.com.

Edited by Karen Hill.

The "Born Crucified" excerpt comes from Max Lucado's *Just Like Jesus.* Used by permission of W Publishing Group.

Library of Congress Cataloging-in-Publication Data

Lucado, Max
    The Christmas Cross : a story about finding your own way home for the holidays / by Max Lucado
        p. cm.
    ISBN 978-1-5955-4060-7 (repackage)
    ISBN 978-0-8499-1768-4 (hardcover)
    ISBN 978-0-8499-1546-8 (orig. hardcover)
    1. Christmas stories, American   I. Title
    PS3562. U225S4 1998
    813'.54—dc21   98-34380
                                                        CIP

Printed in the United States of America

08 09 10 11 12 QW 9 8 7 6 5 4 3 2

Dedicated to all single parents.
May God give you strength.

FOREWORD

In the mystery of Christmas, we find its majesty. The mystery of how God became flesh, why he chose to come, and how much he must love his people.

Such mysteries can never be solved, just as love can never be diagrammed. Christmas is best pondered, not with logic, but imagination.

This book contains Christmas imaginings. Since its release in 1998, God has used it to stretch minds and warm hearts. My earnest prayer is that it does both for you.

—Max Lucado

I lowered my windshield visor, both to block the afternoon sun and retrieve the photo. With one hand holding the picture and the other on the steering wheel, I inched my rental car down Main Street.

Clearwater, Texas, was ready for Christmas. The sky was bright winter blue. A breeze just crisp enough for a jacket swayed the large plastic bells hanging beneath the lamp lights. Aluminum garlands connected the power poles, and Frosty the Snowman chased his hat on the Dairy Kreem window. Even the pick-up truck in front of me had a wreath hanging on

Max Lucado

its tailgate. This central Texas town was ready for Christmas. But I wasn't.

I wanted to be back in Chicago. I wanted to be home. But things weren't so good at home. Meg and I had fought. Weeks of suppressed tension had exploded the day before. Same song, second verse.

"You promised to spend more time at home," she said.

"You promised not to nag," I replied.

She says I work too much. I say we've got bills to pay. She feels neglected. I feel frustrated. Finally, she told me we needed

some—what was the word? Oh yeah, we needed some "space". . . some time apart, and I agreed. I had an assignment in Dallas anyway, so why not go to Texas a few days early?

So, it was the fight with Meg that got me to Texas. But it was the photo that led me to Clearwater. My dad had received it in the mail. No return address. No letter. Just this photo: a black-and-white image of a large, stone building. I could barely make out the words on the sign in front: Clearwater Lutheran Church.

Dad had no clue what the photo meant or who had sent it. We were familiar with the

town, of course. Clearwater was where I was born and adopted. But we never lived there. My only previous visit had been when I was fresh out of college and curious. I had spent a day walking around asking questions, but that was twenty years ago. I hadn't been back since. And I wouldn't have returned now except Meg needed "space" and I could use an answer about the photo.

I pulled over to the side of the road and stopped in front of a two-story brick courthouse. Cardboard cutouts of Santa and his reindeer teetered on the lawn. I lowered my window

and showed the photo to a couple of aging cowboys leaning against the side of a truck.

"Ever seen this place?" I asked.

They smiled at each other and one cowboy spoke. "If you've got a strong arm, you could throw a rock from here and hit it."

He instructed me to turn right past the courthouse and turn right again. And when I did, I saw it. The church in the photo.

My preconceived notion of a small-town church didn't match what I was seeing. I had always imagined a small, white-framed building with a simple belfry over the entrance.

Something like an overgrown dollhouse. Not so, this structure. The white stone walls and tall steel roof spoke of permanence. Long wings extended to the right and left. I had expressed similar surprise when Dad first showed me the photo. But he had reminded me about the large number of German immigrants in the area—immigrants who took both their faith and their crafts seriously.

I parked in one of the diagonal spots near the church. In deference to the December chill, I put on my jacket, then grabbed my cap and gloves as I got out of the car. Tall elms

canopied the wide sidewalk to the church steps. To my right was a brick sign bearing the name of the church in bronzed letters. On the left side of the church a nativity scene stood on the lawn. Although I didn't pause to examine it, I was impressed by its quality. Like the church, it seemed sturdy and detailed. I made a mental note to examine it later.

A sudden gust of wind at my back forced me to use two hands to pull open the thick wooden doors. Organ music welcomed me as I entered. With cap and gloves in hand, I stopped in the foyer. It was empty. From the

look of things, it wouldn't be empty for long. The church had the appearance of a service about to happen. Large red and white poinsettias sat on the floor flanking the foyer doors. A guest book, open and ready to receive the names of visitors, rested on a podium. Garlands of pine looped across a large window that separated the foyer from the sanctuary.

I opened the doors and took a step inside. As I did, the volume of the organ music rose a notch. A long, carpeted aisle bisected the auditorium, and a vaulted ceiling rose above it. Evening sunlight, tinted red by stained glass, cast long rectangles across the empty pews. An advent wreath hung on the pulpit, and unlit candles sat on the window sills. The only movements were those of a silver-haired woman rehearsing on the organ and an older fellow placing programs in hymnal racks. Neither noticed my entrance.

Max Lucado

I spoke in the direction of the man. "Is there a service tonight?"

No response.

"Excuse me," I said a little louder, "is there a service tonight?"

He looked up at me through wire-rimmed glasses, cocked his head, and cupped a hand behind his ear.

"I said, 'Is there a Christmas service tonight?!'" I felt awkward raising my voice in the sanctuary.

"No, we don't need a linen service, thank you. We wash our own towels."

I chuckled to myself and, when I did, I
noticed how good it felt and how long it'd
been. "No," I repeated, walking in his
direction. "I was asking about the Christmas
Eve service."

"Hold on." He turned toward the organist.
"Sarah, can you hold up for a moment? We've
got a salesman calling on us."

Sarah obliged, and the man looked at me
again. "There now, what did you say?"

I repeated the question a fourth time.

"You planning to come?" he asked.

"I'm thinking about it."

Max Lucado

11

"Good thing God was more convicted than you."

"What?"

"God didn't just give it thought, you know. He did it. He came."

Spunky, this guy. Short and square bodied. Not fat, but barrel chested. "Maintenance" was stenciled over the pocket of his gray shirt. He stepped out from the pews, walked up the aisle, and stood in front of me. As blue eyes sized me up, his stubby fingers scratched a thick crop of white hair.

"Been a while since you've been in church?"

His accent didn't sound pure Texan. Midwestern, maybe?

I suppose I wasn't cloaking my discomfort too well. It had been a while since I'd been in a church. And I did feel awkward being there, so I sidestepped the comment.

"I came because of this." I produced the photo. He looked down through his bifocals and smiled.

"My, the trees have grown." Looking up at me, he asked, "Where you from?"

"Chicago. I'm a journalist."

I don't always say that, but the old fellow

seemed to be grading me, and I felt I could use a few points. If I earned any, he didn't say.

"You ought to be home for Christmas, son."

"Well, I'd like to, but I have an assignment and . . ."

"And your work has you out of town on Christmas Eve?"

Who are you to grill me? I started to ask, but didn't. Instead, I picked up a worship program and looked at it. "Yeah, being home would be nice, but since I'm here I thought I'd . . ."

"Six o'clock."

"What?"

"The service. It starts at six." He extended a hand in my direction. "Joe's my name. Forgive me for being nosy. It's just that a man away from his wife . . ."

"How did you . . ."

"Your finger. I can see where your ring was. Must have been recent."

I looked at my hand and thumbed the line. Angry at Meg, I'd stuck my wedding band in my pocket on the plane. "Yeah, recent," I shrugged. "Listen, I'll be back at six. I'd like to meet the pastor. I've got some things to do

now, though," I said, putting the program back in the hymnal rack.

What a lie, I mumbled to myself as I turned. I had absolutely nothing to do and nowhere to go. Joe watched me as I walked down the aisle. At least I think he did. Only when I reached the foyer did I hear him whistling and working again. As I gave the auditorium one final look, Sarah resumed her rehearsal. I turned to go outside. The wooden doors were still stubborn. I paused on the steps, put on my cap, and looked around.

$\mathcal{S}$everal people stepped into the corner drugstore. Last-minute shoppers, I thought. A fellow with a western hat gave me a wave as he walked past. Not far behind him a woman clutching a shopping bag of gifts in one hand and a youngster's hand in the other scurried into the Smart Shoppe across the street. In the adjacent lot, cars encircled Happy's Cafe. Through snow-painted windows I could see families at the tables. I sighed at the sight of them, struck by the irony of my plight. All alone forty years ago. All alone today.

I took a deep breath and started down the

Max Lucado

steps, again noticing the manger scene to my right. Curious, I headed toward it, the yellow grass cracking beneath my feet as I walked.

Lowering my head, I entered the stable and studied the figures, obviously hand-carved, hand-painted. They were the largest ones I'd seen. The shepherds, though kneeling, were over two-feet tall. I was struck by the extraordinary detail of the carvings. Joseph's beard wasn't just painted on; it was carved into the wood. His hand, resting on the manger, was complete with knuckles and fingernails. Mary knelt on the other side, her hand

brushing hair back from her forehead as she looked at her son.

One shepherd had his hand on the shoulder of another. Their faces had a leather hue and a convincing look of awe. Even the wise men were unique, one gesturing at the infant, another holding the bridle of a camel, and the third reverently placing a gift before the crib.

Two cows dozed on folded legs. A sheep and three lambs occupied the space on the other side. I bent down and ran my hand over the white, varnished back of the smallest lamb.

"You won't find a set like this anywhere."

Max Lucado

Startled, I stood and bumped my head on the roof of the stable. I turned. It was Joe. He'd donned a baseball cap and jacket.

"Each figure hand-carved," he continued, "right down to the last eyelash and hoof. Mr. Ottolman donated the manger scene to the church. It's been the pride of the city ever since."

"Mr. Autobahn?" I asked.

"Ottolman. A woodworker from Germany. This was his penance."

"Penance?"

"Self-imposed. He was drunk the night his wife went into labor. So drunk he wrecked the

car while driving her to the hospital. The baby survived, but the mother didn't make it."

I squatted down and put my hand on Mary's face. I could feel the individual hairs of her eyebrows. Then I ran my finger across the smile on her lips.

"He spent the better part of a decade doing the work. He made a living building furniture and spent his time raising Carmen and carving these figures."

"Carmen was his daughter?"

"Yes, the girl who survived. Let me show you something."

Joe removed his hat, either out of reverence for the crèche or regard for the low roof, and knelt before the crib. I joined him. The grass was cold beneath our knees.

"Pull the blanket off the infant Jesus and look at his chest."

I did as he asked. Evening shadows made it difficult to see, but I could make out the figure of a small cross furrowed into the wood. I ran my finger over the groove. Maybe a couple of inches long and half that wide, deep and wide enough for the tip of my finger.

"For nearly ten years a wooden scarlet cross sat in that space."

He could see the question on my face and explained. "Ottolman wasn't a believer when he began. But something about carving the face of the Messiah . . ." His voice drifted off for a minute as he touched the tiny chin. "Somewhere in the process he became interested. He went to church, this very church, and asked the pastor all about Jesus. Reverend Jackson told him not just about the birth but about the death of Christ and invited him to Sunday worship. He went.

Max Lucado

"He took little Carmen with him. She was only a toddler. The two sat on the front pew and heard their first sermon. 'Born Crucified' was the name of the lesson. The message changed his life. He told everyone about it."

Joe smiled and stepped out from under the roof, then stood in the grass, his breath puffing clouds in the cold.

"He used to retell the message to Carmen every night. He'd sit her on her bed and pretend he was the pastor." At this point Joe lowered his voice and took on a pulpit rhythm.

"'Baby Jesus was born to be crucified. He came not just for Bethlehem but for Calvary—not just to live with us, but to die for us. Born with love in his eyes and the cross in his heart. He was born crucified.'"

Joe's blue eyes blazed and his meaty fist punched the air, as if he were the reverend making the point.

"So you knew him?"

"I did."

"And Carmen?"

"Yes," he sighed. "Very well."

Still on my knees, I turned back to the

baby and touched the indentation left by the cross. He chuckled behind me and said, "Ottolman told some of the members about his idea for the carving and they thought it was crazy. 'Baby Jesus doesn't wear a cross,' they said. But he insisted. And one Christmas when he brought the figures out and set them on the lawn, there was a wooden scarlet cross in the baby's chest. Some people made a stink about it, but the reverend, he didn't mind."

"And the cross, where is it now? Is it lost?"

Joe put his hands in his pockets and stared

off into space, then looked back at me. "No, it's not lost. Come with me." He turned and walked toward the church doors. I followed him into the building.

O*ver here," he called as I stood* in the entrance, letting my eyes adjust to the darkening room.

I took off my cap, and Joe led me through a door off the right side of the foyer, down a long hall. We passed a row of portraits, apparently a gallery of pastors. I followed him around a corner until we stood in front of a door marked "Library." There must have been thirty keys hanging from a chain on Joe's belt. One of them unlocked the door. After he turned on the lights, we crossed the room to a corner where a stand held a thick scrapbook. In a

couple of turns the old man found what he was looking for.

"This article appeared in our paper on Christmas Day, 1958."

The yellowed newsprint told the story:

Stolen Baby Jesus Home for Christmas

He was silent as I read the first paragraph:

"Mr. Ottolman must have been pretty angry."

"No, he wasn't upset."

"But his baby was taken."

"Finish the article, and I'll get us some coffee."

As he left the room, I continued reading:

The baby Jesus, part of a set hand-carved by a local woodworker, was taken from the Clearwater Lutheran Church sometime yesterday. The minister had posted a sign pleading for the babe's return. "At last night's Christmas Eve service," Reverend Jackson reported, "we had special prayers for the baby. With the homecoming of Baby Jesus, the prayers were answered."

I was staring at the photograph attached to the article when Joe returned with two

Max Lucado

Styrofoam cups of coffee. "Look closely," he said. "See anything missing?"

"The cross?"

Joe nodded. "Won't you sit down?"

We sat on either side of a long mahogany table. Joe took a sip of coffee and began.

"Nineteen fifty-eight. Carmen was eighteen. Lively, lovely girl, she was. Ottolman did his best to raise her, but she had her own ways. Would have been good had he remarried, but he never did.

"Told people a man only has room in his heart for one woman; Carmen was his. She was

everything to him. Took her fishing on Saturdays and picked her up after school. Every Sunday the two sat on the front pew of this church and sang. My how they sang.

"And every night he would pray. He'd thank God for his good grace and then beg God, 'Take care of my Carmen, Lord. Take care of my Carmen.'"

Joe looked away as if remembering her. For the first time I heard conversation in the hall. Parishioners were beginning to arrive. Somewhere a choir was rehearsing. Just as I found myself hoping Joe wouldn't stop his

story, he continued. "Carmen's mother was a beauty from Mexico. And Carmen had every ounce of her beauty. Dark skin, black hair, and eyes that could melt your soul. She couldn't walk down Main Street without being whistled at.

"This bothered Ottolman. He was from the old school, you know. As she got older, he got stricter. It was for her own good, but she couldn't see that. He went too far, Ottolman did. He went too far. Told her to stay away from boys and to stay away from anyplace where boys were. And she did, mostly.

"Early in the summer of '58, Carmen discovered she was pregnant. She kept it from her father as long as she could. Being small of stature, she hid it quite well. But by December it was obvious. When he found out, he did something very, very bad. For the rest of his life he regretted that December night."

Joe's tone shifted from one of telling to one of questioning. "Why do people do the thing they swear they'll never do?"

I wasn't sure if he expected me to answer or not, but before I could, he sighed and continued.

Max Lucado

"Well, Carmen's dad got mad and he got drunk. He wasn't a bad man; he just did a bad thing. He forgot his faith. And . . ." Joe shook his head, "you're not going to believe this. Just before Christmas, he and Carmen had a wreck. Twice in one lifetime the man wrecked a car carrying the woman he loved."

Joe stopped again, I suppose to let me mull over what he'd said. He was right; I found it hard to believe. How could a man repeat such a tragic event? But then, it occurred to me that I was doing the same with Meg.

Swearing to do better, only to fail again . . .

and again. Maybe it wasn't so impossible after all.

"Go on," I urged. "What happened to them?"

"Ottolman came out of it OK, but Carmen was hurt, badly hurt. They took her to the hospital where her daddy sat by her bed every single minute. 'Oh, Jesus,' he would pray, 'take care of my Carmen. Don't let her die.' The doctors told him they would have to take the baby as soon as Carmen was stable.

"The night passed and Carmen slept. Ottolman sat by her side and Carmen slept.

She slept right up until Christmas Eve morning. Then she woke up. Her first words were a question: 'Daddy, has my baby come?'

"He bounded out of his chair and took her hand. 'No, Carmen, but the baby is fine. The doctors are sure the baby is fine.'

"'Where am I?'

"He knelt at her bedside. 'You're in the hospital, darling. It's Christmas Eve.' He put her hand on his cheek and told her what had happened. He told her about his drinking and the accident and he began to weep. 'I'm so sorry, Carmen. I'm so sorry.'

"Then Carmen did a wonderful thing. She stroked her father's head and said, 'It's OK, Papa. It's OK. I love you.'

"He leaned forward and put his face in the crook of her neck and wept. Carmen cried, too. She put her arm around her daddy's neck and cried.

"Neither said anything for the longest time; they just held each other, each tear washing away the hurt. Finally Carmen spoke: 'Papa, will the baby come before Christmas?'

"'I don't know, princess.'

"'I'd like that.' She smiled, her brown eyes

twinkling. 'I'd like very much to have a baby to hold this Christmas Eve.'

"Those were her final words. She closed her eyes to rest. But she never woke up."

*J*oe's eyes misted and he looked at the floor. I started to say he didn't have to tell me the rest of the story, but when he lifted his head, he was smiling—a soft, tender smile. "It was around lunchtime when Ottolman had the idea. 'You want to sleep with your baby, Carmen?' he whispered in her ear. 'I'll get you your baby.'

"For the first time in weeks he left the hospital. Out the door and across the street he marched. He walked straight past the courthouse and slowed his pace only when he neared the church. For a long time he stared at

the crèche from across the street—the very crèche you saw this afternoon. He was planning something. He took a deep breath and crossed the church lawn.

"He began adjusting the manger scene, like he was inspecting the figures, looking for cracks or marks. Anyone passing by would have thought nothing of Mr. Ottolman examining his handiwork. And no one passing by would have seen that when he left, there was no baby Jesus in the manger.

"Only an hour later, when the reverend was showing the display to his grandchildren, did

The Christmas Child

anyone notice. By then, the baby with the scarlet cross was wrapped in a blanket and nestled under the covers next to Carmen.

"Her final wish was granted. She held a baby on Christmas Eve."

For a long time neither Joe nor I spoke. He sat leaning forward, hands folded between his knees. He wasn't there. Nor was I. We were both in the world of Ottolman and Carmen and the sculptured baby in the manger. Though I'd never seen their faces, I could see them in my mind. I could see Ottolman pulling back the hospital sheets and placing the

infant Jesus next to his daughter. And I could see him setting a chair next to the bed, taking Carmen's hand in his . . . and waiting.

I broke the silence with one word: "Carmen?"

"She died two days later."

"The baby?"

"He came, early. But he came."

"Mr. Ottolman?"

"He stayed on in Clearwater. Still lives here, as a matter of fact. But he never went back to his house. He couldn't face the emptiness."

"So what happened to him?"

Joe cleared his throat. "Well, the church took him in—gave him a job and a little room at the back of the sanctuary."

Until that moment, until he spoke those words, the possibility had not entered my mind. I leaned forward and looked directly into his face. "Who are you?"

"You have her eyes, you know," he whispered.

"You mean, Carmen was . . ."

"Yes. Your mother. And I'm, well, I'm . . . your . . ."

". . . Grandfather?"

Max Lucado

45

His chin began to tremble as he told me, "I've made some big mistakes, son. And I pray I'm not making another one right now. I just wanted you to know what happened. And I wanted to see you while I still could."

As I struggled to understand, he reached into his shirt pocket. He removed an object, placed it in my palm, and folded my hand around it. "I've been keeping this for you. She would want you to have it." And I opened my hand to see a cross—a small, wooden, scarlet cross.

*L*ater that evening I called Meg from my room. I told her about Carmen, Ottolman, and the family I'd discovered. "Were you angry at Joe?" she asked.

"Funny," I said, "of all the emotions that flooded me in that church library, anger wasn't one of them. Shock? Yes. Disbelief? Of course. But anger, no. Joe's assessment of himself sounds fair. He is a good man who did a very bad thing."

There was a long pause. Meg and I both knew what needed to be discussed next. She found a way to broach it. "What about me?" Her voice was soft. "Are you angry at me?"

With no hesitation, I responded, "No, there's been too much anger between us."

She agreed. "If Carmen forgave Joe, don't you suppose we could do the same for each other?"

"I'll be home tomorrow," I told my wife.

"I've got a better idea," she replied.

So Meg flew to Texas to be with us.

She made it to Clearwater in time to have dinner with two men who, by virtue of mistakes and mercy and Christmas miracles, had found their way home for the holidays.

LETTER FROM
THE PUBLISHER

Dear Reader,

As a special feature of this new edition of *The Christmas Child*, we have included a passage from one of Max Lucado's most beloved non-fiction books, *Just Like Jesus*. While the heart-warming story you just finished was about fictional events that occurred one Christmas in the small town of Clearwater, Texas, this excerpt from *Just Like Jesus* delves into the facts of the first Christmas . . . the facts of the living, breathing Christmas Child. You'll find that the core message of the two stories is the same, but this excerpt will give you a new perspective on the story you just read and a deeper understanding of the love that abounds at Christmastime.

Max Lucado

Take a moment to savor the two, and perhaps even a moment to think through some of the discussion questions found at the back of this book. We hope you'll grow even closer to Jesus as you savor the story of the Christmas Child and consider what the Son of Man did for us all on that very first Christmas day—as a babe in the manger.

Publisher,
WestBow Press

BORN CRUCIFIED

*S*ent from heaven to hang on a cross: the baby born crucified. Every minute of his life moving him a heartbeat nearer to his ultimate encounter with our sin and heaven's redemption. Why? Because of you and because of me. Because of love . . . a limitless love reaching across time for the sake of eternal grace. The first Christmas child, sought by shepherds and worshiped by wise men.

And the wise still seek him. Not in an empty manger. Not on a distant cross. The baby born crucified? He is as near as your next prayer.

The world has never known a heart so pure,

Max Lucado

a character so flawless. His spiritual hearing was so keen he never missed a heavenly whisper. His mercy so abundant he never missed a chance to forgive. No lie left his lips, no distraction marred his vision. He touched when others recoiled. He endured when others quit.

I urge you to look for him . . . to see Jesus.

The shepherds can tell us what it means to see Jesus. For them it wasn't enough to see the angels. You'd think it would have been. Night sky shattered with light. Stillness erupting with song. Simple shepherds roused from their sleep and raised to their feet by a choir of angels:

Excerpt from Just Like Jesus

"Glory to God in the highest!" Never had these men seen such splendor.

But it wasn't enough to see the angels. The shepherds wanted to see the one who sent the angels. Since they wouldn't be satisfied until they saw him, you can trace the long line of Jesus-seekers to a person of the pasture who said, "Let's go . . . Let's see" (Luke 2:15).

Not far behind the shepherds was a man named Simeon. Luke tells us Simeon was a good man who served in the temple during the time of Christ's birth. Luke also tells us, "Simeon had been told by the Holy Spirit that

he would not die before he saw the Christ
promised by the Lord" (Luke 2:26). This
prophecy was fulfilled only a few days after the
shepherds saw Jesus. Somehow Simeon knew
that the blanketed bundle he saw in Mary's
arms was the Almighty God. And for Simeon,
seeing Jesus was enough. Now he was ready to
die. Some don't want to die until they've seen
the world. Simeon's dream was not so timid.
He didn't want to die until he had seen the
maker of the world. He had to see Jesus.

He prayed: "God, you can now release your
servant; release me in peace as you promised.

With my own eyes I've seen your salvation" (Luke 2:29-30 MSG).

The Magi had the same desire. Like Simeon, they wanted to see Jesus. Like the shepherds, they were not satisfied with what they saw in the night sky. Not that the star wasn't spectacular. Not that the star wasn't historical. To be a witness of the blazing orb was a privilege, but for the Magi, it wasn't enough. It wasn't enough to see the light over Bethlehem; they had to see the Light of Bethlehem. It was him they came to see.

And they succeeded! They all succeeded.

Max Lucado

More remarkable than their diligence was Jesus' willingness. Jesus wanted to be seen! Whether they came from the pasture or the palace, whether they lived in the temple or among the sheep, whether their gift was of gold or honest surprise . . . they were welcomed. Search for one example of one person who desired to see the infant Jesus and was turned away. You won't find it.

You will find examples of those who didn't seek him. Those, like King Herod, who were content with less. Those, like the religious leaders, who preferred to read about him than

to see him. The ratio between those who missed him and those who sought him is thousands to one. But the ratio between those who sought him and those who found him is one to one. All who sought him found him. Long before the words were written, this promise was proven: "God . . . rewards those who truly want to find him" (Heb. 11:6).

The examples continue. Consider John and Andrew. They, too, were rewarded. For them it wasn't enough to listen to John the Baptist. Most would have been content to serve in the shadow of the world's most famous evangelist.

Max Lucado

Could there be a better teacher? Only one. And when John and Andrew saw him, they left John the Baptist and followed Jesus. Note the request they made.

"Rabbi," they asked, "where are you staying?" (John 1:38). Pretty bold request. They didn't ask Jesus to give them a minute or an opinion or a message or a miracle. They asked for his address. They wanted to hang out with him. They wanted to know him. They wanted to know what caused his head to turn and his heart to burn and his soul to yearn. They wanted to study his eyes and

follow his steps. They wanted to see him. They wanted to know what made him laugh and if he ever got tired. And most of all, they wanted to know, could Jesus be who John said he was—and if he is, what on earth is God doing on the earth? You can't answer such a question by talking to his cousin; you've got to talk to the man himself.

Jesus' answer to the disciples? "Come and see" (v. 39). He didn't say, "Come and glance," or "Come and peek." He said, "Come and see." Bring your bifocals and binoculars. This is no time for side-glances or

occasional peeks. "Let us fix our eyes on Jesus, the author and perfecter of our faith" (Heb. 12:2 NIV).

The disciple fixes his eyes on the Savior.

That's what Matthew did. Matthew was converted at work. According to his résumé, he was a revenue consultant for the government. According to his neighbors, he was a crook. He kept a tax booth and a hand extended at the street corner. That's where he was the day he saw Jesus. "Follow me," the Master said, and Matthew did. And in the very next verse we find Jesus sitting at Matthew's dining room

table. "Jesus was having dinner at Matthew's house" (Matt. 9:10).

A curbside conversion couldn't satisfy his heart, so Matthew took Jesus home. Something happens over a dinner table that doesn't happen over an office desk. Take off the tie, heat up the grill, break out the sodas, and spend the evening with the suspender of the stars. "You know, Jesus, forgive me for asking but I've always wanted to know . . ."

Again, though the giving of the invitation is impressive, the acceptance is more so. Didn't matter to Jesus that Matthew was a thief.

Max Lucado

Didn't matter to Jesus that Matthew had built a split-level house with the proceeds of extortion. What did matter was that Matthew wanted to know Jesus, and since God "rewards those who truly want to find him" (Heb. 11:6), Matthew was rewarded with the presence of Christ in his home.

Of course, it only made sense that Jesus spent time with Matthew. After all, Matthew was a top draft pick, shoulder-tapped to write the first book of the New Testament. Jesus hangs out with only the big guys like Matthew and Andrew and John. Right?

Excerpt from Just Like Jesus

May I counter that opinion with an example? Zacchaeus was far from a big guy. He was small, so small he couldn't see over the crowd that lined the street the day Jesus came to Jericho. Of course the crowd might have let him elbow up to the front, except that he, like Matthew, was a tax collector. But he, like Matthew, had a hunger in his heart to see Jesus.

It wasn't enough to stand at the back of the crowd. It wasn't enough to peer through a cardboard telescope. It wasn't enough to listen to someone else describe the parade of the

Messiah. Zacchaeus wanted to see Jesus with his own eyes.

So he went out on a limb. Clad in a three-piece Armani suit and brand-new Italian loafers, he shimmied up a tree in hopes of seeing Christ.

I wonder if you would be willing to do the same. Would you go out on a limb to see Jesus? Not everyone would. In the same Bible where we read about Zacchaeus crawling across the limb, we read about a young ruler. Unlike Zacchaeus, the crowd parted to make room for him. He was the . . . ahem . . . rich,

young ruler. Upon learning that Jesus was in the area, he called for the limo, cruised across town, and approached the carpenter. Please note the question he had for Jesus: "Teacher, what good thing must I do to have life forever?" (Matt. 19:16).

Bottom line sort of fellow, this ruler. No time for formalities or conversations. "Let's get right to the issue. Your schedule is busy; so is mine. Tell me how I can get saved, and I'll leave you alone."

There was nothing wrong with his question, but there was a problem with his heart.

Contrast his desire with that of Zacchaeus: "Can I make it up that tree?"

Or John and Andrew: "Where are you staying?"

Or Matthew: "Can you spend the evening?"

Or Simeon: "Can I stay alive until I see him?"

Or the Magi: "Saddle up the camels. We aren't stopping until we find him."

Or the shepherd: "Let's go . . . Let's see."

See the difference? The rich, young ruler wanted medicine. The others wanted the Physician. The ruler wanted an answer to the quiz. They wanted the teacher. He was in a

hurry. They had all the time in the world. He settled for a cup of coffee at the drive-through window. They wouldn't settle for anything less than a full-course meal at the banquet table. They wanted more than salvation. They wanted the Savior. They wanted to see Jesus.

They were earnest in their search. One translation renders Hebrews 11:6: "God . . . rewards those who earnestly seek him" (NIV).

Another reads: "God rewards those who search for him" (PHILLIPS).

And another: "God . . . rewards those who sincerely look for him" (TLB).

Max Lucado

I like the King James translation: "He is a rewarder of them that diligently seek him."

Diligently—what a great word. Be diligent in your search. Be hungry in your quest, relentless in your pilgrimage. Let this hour be but one of hundreds in which you seek him. Step away from the puny pursuits of possessions and positions, and seek your king.

Don't be satisfied with angels. Don't be content with stars in the sky. Seek him out as the shepherds did. Long for him as Simeon did. Worship him as the wise men did. Do as John and Andrew did: ask for his address. Do

as Matthew: invite Jesus into your house. Imitate Zacchaeus. Risk whatever it takes to see Christ.

God rewards those who seek him. Not those who seek doctrine or religion or systems or creeds. Many settle for these lesser passions, but the reward goes to those who settle for nothing less than Jesus himself. And what is the reward? What awaits those who seek Jesus? Nothing short of the heart of Jesus. "And as the Spirit of the Lord works within us, we become more and more like him" (2 Cor. 3:18 TLB).

Can you think of a greater gift than to be

like Jesus? Jesus felt no guilt; God wants to banish yours. Jesus had no bad habits; God wants to remove yours. Jesus had no fear of death; God wants you to be fearless. Jesus had kindness for the diseased and mercy for the rebellious and courage for the challenges.

God wants you to have the same.

DISCUSSION GUIDE

1.) When you see the manger scene at Christmas, or read the account of Jesus' birth in the book of Matthew, what kind of feelings do you experience?

2.) When Joe asks the main character if he will come to the church service that evening and he gives a noncommittal reply, Joe responds with "Good thing God was more convicted than you." What do you think Joe is implying with that statement? Do you think it's a common problem for people to not be able to commit to God, to their churches, to their families?

3.) Joe quickly observes and comments about the fact that this stranger who has come into the church still has a white line on his finger from his wedding band. Do you think Joe's comment is too forward or does his perceptiveness allow him to address a source of obvious pain?

4.) When the man walks out of the church, he thinks about the fact that he was "all alone forty years ago. All alone today." The difference is that he is alone today as a result of his own actions. What could he have done differently to avoid the feelings of aloneness that he has? Is he even truly alone?

5.) Does the reconciliation that happened between the narrator and his wife, Meg, encourage you to seek or give forgiveness in a relationship that is important to you?

6.) In the same way that Joe Ottolman made the same mistake twice, what in your life seems to be a reoccurring experience that you would like for God to help you overcome?

7.) Mr. Ottolman carved the nativity set for the church as his self-imposed penance. What do you think is the significance of choosing that particular act of penance for himself?

8.) When Mr. Ottolman carved the nativity scene, he placed the scarlet cross on the baby's chest. Why was it so significant to him that the baby Jesus was "born crucified"?

9.) How was Joe willing to take risks and abandon his pride like some of the biblical characters discussed in the "Born Crucified" sermon?

10.) Why did Joe send the picture of the church at that particular time? Why not twenty years earlier? What can we learn from the way Joe handled their reunion?

11.) In what ways was Joe Ottolman living out the words of Hebrews 11:6?

Without faith no one can please God. Anyone who comes to God must believe that he is real and that he rewards those who truly want to find him.

12.) Carmen made one last request before she passed away. How was her request similar to that of the disciple Matthew's request?

13.) The two men, "by virtue of mistakes and mercy and Christmas miracles, had found their way home for the holidays." What does it mean to be "home for the holidays"? Is it more a matter of place or a matter of the heart?

14.) In the "Born Crucified" section, Max Lucado states, "Search for one example of one person who desired to see the infant Jesus and was turned away. You won't find it." Is this still true today? What response have you found when you desired to see Jesus?

15.) Both Simeon (his account is told in the book of Luke) and Joe are men who have dedicated the remainder of their lives serving in the Lord's house. How else might these two men be similar?

❋

16.) The "Born Crucified" section asks the question, "Would you go out on a limb to see Jesus?" Would you? If so, what limbs have you clung to in order to see Christ?

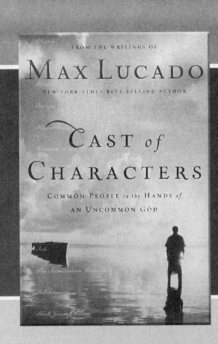

If you love the story,
experience the movie!

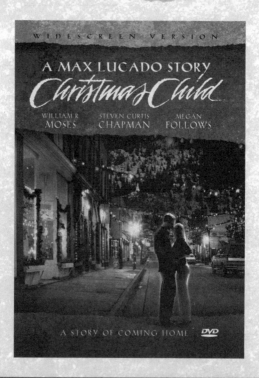

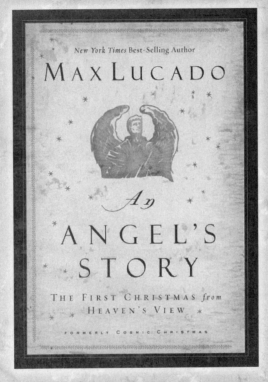

A Heart-Warming Novel From
a Master Storyteller

New York Times Best-Selling Author

MAX LUCADO

The
CHRISTMAS
CANDLE

Available Now